LOVE LAND

PETER D. GRIFFIN

Paintings by John Schlereth

PASSAGES
PUBLICATIONS

Love Land
© 2016 by Peter Griffin

Published by Passages Publications

Cover and book design by Tom Greensfelder

ISBN SBN-10: 0-692-77925-6
ISBN-13: 978-0-692-77925-5

Printed in the United States of America

FOREWORD

It is an odd thing that in considering a name
for this collection of poems that I immediately,
without any internal deliberation, decided to call
it *Love Land*. I am an inveterate second guesser so
my certainty on this, a most revealing of decisions,
was out of character. Let me first concede that it
is a silly, pretentious name casted by an amateur
who has little right to the currency of this greatest
of emotions. But, to me, the title is wholly
appropriate. I considered the corners of my life
every day, the ebb and flow of disagreements raised
and forgotten, the consistency of my family life
locked in the reassuring cocoon of the Connecticut
suburbs, and my decidedly professional existence as
a physician supporting this enterprise and yet in all,
at all times, love has always been the catch basin of
my life. It is what I want at any given moment; it
is the thought that catches me while doing dishes,
brushing my teeth, driving to work.

I think that the title would play better if I were a
more prepossessing figure: a football player, boxer
— a man of physical talents. That is, to contrast
a softer side of a harder character, a revelation of
humanity that must exist in all of us no matter
who, observed always even in the most hard-bitten.
But I am perhaps like you — "politic, cautious,
sometimes overly meticulous; full of high sentence
but a bit obtuse." The contrast between a middle-
aged physician and a book of poems, especially
love poems, does not seem like too big a stretch

(there are Wallace Stevens and William Carlos Williams after all) but I can already hear the snickering beginning in the foot lights — so be it.

The book is divided into two sections: *Love* poems and *Others*. But in *Others*, there is, of course, more of the same — my soul is bleeding with memory and desire. My friends and family will be able to readily trace my life, and my love for them, through many of the *Other* poems. My parents, siblings and friends are represented, some more obviously so: *Margaret* (my mother); *Father*, and *Cole DeWald* to name a few. *Childhood* was a dedication to the boys of my neighborhood who defined those wonderful years and made me begin to understand, in my first childish way, love as it exists outside of family. True children (and adults) can hate as ferociously as they can love. Being brought up Irish Catholic, perhaps the darker side of these intense feelings was more manifest in me and my mates at St. Paul. Though I couldn't articulate it then, however, I can now: Red Rover, Red Rover and all the other blacktop games, second base in the sand lot behind St. Paul's, lunch pails and 10 cent ice cream bars, Sister Katerina — all run over me — are carried with me and enjoyed as the subjects of my first loves.

I remember later in grade school crying uncontrollably and beating back an incredulous crowd of buddies who were torturing (mercilessly, as children will do) another classmate in the gym locker room. He was a small, sensitive boy who missed many days of school because of "illness." He lived alone with his mother. He had no friends but he caused no problems. My emotional defense of him surprised even me as I had never spoken a word to him before this or after, but I realize now, almost 50 years later, that it was my love of him, the love of an innocent — "the notion of some infinitely gentle, infinitely suffering thing" — that drove me.

I see all children in this way now. My son has caused this great revelation in me for it is in his company that I return, after so many years of neglect, to these memories of my earliest friends and the emotions that they engendered in the soft clay of my young consciousness. To be a child is to be at the heart of this unspoken desire, every day, at all times. It is good that we grow old enough to remember and, perhaps, then to understand the feelings, feeling, that moved us through these warm days of our youth. You may say this is sentimental and that character formation in any child is varied and pushed by a million different impulses, leading to growth, awareness and understanding, etc. I say that — after food and shelter — it is love that we sought then and still seek now.

As adults we see love as the old standby in the wings, to be called upon for only special moments (the goodbye hug, the first and last kiss, the child, the mother, the lover). But it is that which pins us together in our youth and pushes us forward into adulthood. When I am not yelling at traffic or apoplectic discussing politics I have an intense desire to embrace anyone — grocery clerk, train conductor, my patients — just for being human enough to speak with me, the same way I pushed myself into my mother's skirt for that reassuring hug. Once you start throwing away the common irritations of daily life and stop trying to 'find yourself' you'll see — you will find this feeling somewhere in the shallow pools, it's always there, just look.

The *Love* poems are admittedly a life collection but dedicated all to my wife. I wrote *Crucible* long before I met P with no one in particular in mind but this poem, as others, defines our relationship: the pain and travail of catastrophic events we have endured together and the love and hope that has crept up and bloomed through the rumble of those battlefields. Our love was tested from the first day of our marriage, it still prevails. Love untested is not yet real love, only comfort.

I have engaged a Chicago artist and friend, John Schlereth, to complement this poetry with portraits of women from his collection. John describes the energy of his work, his life, as driven by women; he defers to them for all things sensual, lovely, and rational in this world. John, who is a pre-possessing man — a second degree black belt in Okinawan karate by way of 12 years of training with a personality and intellect like a Passaic River flood — has the sensitivity of a woman. That sensitivity and intensity confronts you as you look into the eyes of his models: languorous, innocent, composed and sensual. Their gaze back to you reveals them as women beyond any question of their beauty; their ineffable spirit shows them superior in all ways related to love. That John can capture this, given his limited medium of paint and cardboard, is miraculous and defines him as a great artist. But he would not be able to create this great art without this love of women. I am with John on this, thus, *Love Land*.

PASSAGES

the smell of sage and pine
or some other heaven's breath
curls into the wind
that catches up your coat tails
blows you through
leads you to this hearth where
the shoes of a thousand travelers
wear the wood planks worn with
the heat of their pursuits

men running to balconies,
hot dishes brought in from the cold,
an infant clutched in silent, adoring arms,
a bride stroking a yielding neck,
climbing the threshold,
heading towards the stairs, the stars

memory seeps
through these planks
holds fast to my ankles
the windows far ahead
are filled with the light and promise
something other than this place
where I stand
above the fortress of words

a heart pinned to the floor
will be trampled by all
for all of time

Love Poems

A NEW SUIT

a new suit
woven by the sum beams off the walls
of a hospital somewhere in New Jersey —
cascading light devouring morning smiles
    during rounds
stroked underneath with moon paint
from memories of a younger night in spring
dotted by fire flies
sparkling a chaotic message
never to be learned —
enveloped by night

two pounds of wool
clasped around my chest
a silent hug pressed pleasingly,
my bill fold won't fit
only my hand can press
the apex of my heart
underneath the warm lapel
draped like the arm of a small child
as she leans to whisper a special secret
behind all the glances — stares
from the dinner table,
the other park benches,
the nurse's station —
the special secret
soft collar child song

hugging my neck
brushing the hair away from my ear
wispy laughter soft voice tickling
soft sweet secret child collar song
embracing my neck
so that I am dizzy with anticipation
and fumble with the pants legs
pants that smell like the day of my first
    holy communion
pressed in starch, trimmed in
store new whiteness
gasping at the wonder
of ceremony
the small girl, flowers in hand
next to me
standing beneath the pressure
of sunlight and stain glass
the pants rolling up my shins
clasping my leg
the warmth at my thighs
before I sit
before I fall
awkward, balanced on one foot
trying hard to hold up
this new suit
    — just a new suit
go ahead
try it on

BEAST

I wish to wrestle away
this cruel animal inside me
that eats my strength —
my limbs, my mind,
the days go on numberless

A thousand of these days I offer it
and it buries them casually
I give it all my sight and words —
a lifetime of common learnings —
it steps on these silently
muffling a growl, menacing a canine over a
    quivering lip,
looking for more

If I could
I would make the look in your eyes
into to a knife
hone it with what innocence I have left,
cleave my heart in two,
and let the beast feed on what ever remains

BESIDE ME

Excuse me if I still adore you
The early New England evening,
filled with quiet snow
Has lasted until night fall
And all my hopes wrapped into this moment,
alone at the fireside
Have been proffered, the week's innervating
    work of existence,
Of having tried so hard but resolving to this
    dusk and bourbon
Forgive me if all that is present,
the lives that have left —
the suns that have given up the day,
All that dust on our finger tips that we wash,
and wash from our hands
and try to forget as we are forced to
    remember
All those days,
the days of your laughter, your smile
The days I had left with you to hold my head
    against your chest,
Oh, that you were here again,
oh that this winter storm would leave you at
    our doorway, and
Give you back to me, for this moment,
only this moment beside this fire in front of
    this window,
Beside me, back to me, beside me

BRITTANY

Perhaps I could give you a house by the sea
with green foam rising to the tide of your eyes
    every morning
the sun collecting in sheltered pools on this
    hardscrabble coast
the shells to cover you soft shoulders
the sand to smooth over every other feeling of
    the day

So much is lost in a day
so much heaven to consider drifting away
    like abandoned arms
left to float on these timeless waves
a thousand days and nights you wait for these
    arms to embrace you

You sound the depth of my eyes
you consider every bend of my sleep
and all I can offer you is a house by the sea
with the memory of what is always you close
    to me

BROWN TO BLUE

she is tasseled in twilight
and a smile that lets down from telephone lines
I can not see more of her
for the light in her eyes
brown to blue
she wrestles down my thoughts
brown to blue
she loosens up a main sheet
laughs like tomorrow's children
and sails out

this dance is one I know
brown eyes, rose lips seeking a rhythm in my face
and arms that reach around the side of your
    memory
to a spot where I do not often go —
have forgotten
she places a finger over it and rubs
till I am set against yesterday
back inclined
my arms out searching for her eyes

to rinse this thought
through my hair
feels like the instant before diving
the pelt of water measures up my shoulders
inviting me down to a deeper part of this pool
where brown eyes turn blue

CRUCIBLE

Life at the corners
a glance across the table
there appears to be the center to art

My chances are a smoldering ember
to sprinkle dry twigs
fire the crucible
fire the crucible

GARBAGE

I would be strong
resting in this desert
listening for footfalls

I would carry the weight
of this love
like an obelisk
gazing at the compressed dirt
of your steps

I ask for the holy end
of suffering
your suffering is easy,
unknowing

that the garbage man is at another block
grinding and spitting
is no surprise
he throws another barrel
into the truck
to grind down
into forgotten rubble
enough to fill a countryside
already full
of forsaken love

GLEN ROCK

The empress bends over to kiss
what is left of my visage
I have left the place
that made me trace
the seams of my existence
could there be more to this life than this
smoked filled rooms with memories
and resistance

You are the lark that came at morning
doe eyed, lengthy moment cruelty
I am teenage ambiguity, how I rule

I would like you once again,
I would like to dream over and over
I will use whatever dumb words
will get me close to you
I will fall blank in my code of blue eyed silence
that always worked
created the birth of my place in you

there are birds of spring mocking me
from trees that adorn
a suburban lawn
and life that presents the gifts of
my lifetime

HEART

Heart, oh heart
leave this nest and let the rest
of time become
a final song

What is wrong?
how can my sight of the future
be so gray
where may I grow old
on a sunshine filled beach
where may I smile for everyone
who touches me so lovingly?
where am I to go?

LEAVING

When I leave you it is like I have left myself
one hundred dreams that have sung me to sleep
one thousand pieces of wind that catch me up
on so many tethered nights
caught on your smile, your smile, the father to
    your kiss

I could be more but will never
but I am so much less without you

LUCKY MAN

The lattice of your blouse beneath my gaze
The suggestion of your breast
your breath reaches up to me
before memory sings to my heart

the license of heaven given to
the unworthy paste of a man
who has become lucky —
ablaze
with the good fortune that comes to those
    who wait

MARRIAGE

All hell's fire
sanctifies this desire
to hell we go

the hearth and couch
the peace of Saturday evening
everything that I have seen
would ask me to sing —
the glory of *the Messiah*
and number 414 in your hymnal
Closer To You Oh Lord
songs that take the soul away,
bourbon and Proust
resting on clouds above your beauty
running across an alpine painted poppy field
if you could believe that we are the only ones
to love alone
we can be alone on this mountain top

Groomed and silent
I appear in this poem
dedicated, as always, to you,
the child shall gain my attention,
all of my attention,
a sharp beam of laughter and crying that
I cannot comprehend,
that I cannot deny

except for thoughts of dying and you
He is a fine,
perfect thing —
so lost as a new and now
that I am troubled to demonstrate at
    all against
Him

But after these years
after ecstasy and joy
after bitter bed sheets, restrained
    acceptance,
the ritual conference of marriage
the required compromise
of two with a thin contract of material and
    children
after the common things that bind us
we are still alive with song
lift the lid
the hinges scream
hot as the hinges of Hates
with the negligence of the thing
called love

MONTANA

somewhere between sight and memory
an ember burns on the corner of a woman's laugh
and my life becomes powdered in flame —
all the hard surfaces of my face, faces
wrought from the rifle end of long work days
turn to soft rust
tin cans on a dark green forest bed

the thought distilled from this fire
is a smile
mounted in a cold room,
stripped of tears and real laughter
yet standing alone enough
to wear down edges

I cling to the glint in your eye
and wish to languish against that smile
till I am found vagrant and ask to leave
the furrow of your lip worn smooth,
the promise of you heart
and dressed like a carnival barker
it ask me for more than
my ragged pockets can offer —
I will walk quietly away from the tent
moved aside by the crowd that follows in
festooned with their balloons and candy
they press against the doorway —

their eyes caught on what is colorful but
    common
they will not see what I have captured in a
    single glimpse
set within the bend of my arm
mine, mine alone

the crueler business of hello
is wasted on the wild frontier
of cowboys who tilt their hats
to the vision of rouge and petticoat on
    clapboard streets
they linger in the moment
long enough to forget their sovereign west —
the sun that writes the sky in calico
the doggies as they graze at the mountain's
    foot
they set their legs to saddle
'saddle up young boys'
what is vision has turned to memory
and warm ponies will coat your thighs,
rough leather grace your palms,
long plains fill your eyes,
and before you know it
you are dazed before a campfire
listening to a voice you hardly knew
pass with a smile clouded by dust and
    now ash
As this flame consumes

MY CRANE WIFE

so that you have given your snowy down
from your preening
so more than the life I live
so more than this smile that bleeds from
    my mouth
I am errant and wild for things
You are lovely and sweet at dusk
I am the father of some good thoughts
but I keep them in a cage of straw
tumbling about in my mind

I sail more and look at the skin of the blue
    horizon
I ignore your pain and sweep my bow with
    ocean blue foam
I am looking forward and you are looking
    within for me

You can not keep your secret
I was meant to see it first, to see you first
your lovely plume, your transformed face
I know that you are
settled in a cedar tree near a Hakido mountain
all destroyed: my hands, my face, my desire

PEARLS

Pearls in motion
over the table
the hard, rolling sound of
of a jewel

I let you leave
these before me
to watch their tiny arabesque

a whole string
torn from your neck
pops off
the table's surface
like small hopes
one after the other
to slowly settle
all roll to the edge

PICTURES

In this fading autumn light I shoot pictures
    of you
The cleft in this valley allows the Aspetuck
    and your beauty
To descend, a curtain of water collects in back
    of you with all my desires

You are between dawn and midnight,
shadow and light,
In a place where I cannot have you
Your hair falls back like thick black satin, it
    wraps around my heart
Your smile devours me
in a whirlpool where I am drowning with the
    joy of you
I am yours in this moment
I am snapping pictures like a fool
so high for the want of you,
so lost in the lens that can't leave your face
so lost in you

You don't see the drama behind my camera
you are laughing at me
at the world that you have left in this one
    moment
as you stand between two worlds, a radiant
    and dark woman

The sun asks for you and you smile to
    turn to the Moon
The moon asks for you and you laugh and
    turn to me
I ask for you and you continue to turn,
    and my world turns at each moment

RESCUE

To Lieutenant Timothy Griffin, Scout Pilot, Troop A,
17th Calvary Squadron, the Silver Spurs, and any veteran
who walked into the Lyons VA Hospital Emergency
Department, Lyons, NJ

Small arms fire
dimple the side of this slick
tapping like angry women
at a store window

above
a gun ship
let's slip
10 rounds
from 130 mm cannons
and the Halloween plume of
orange and black
erases this verdant beauty —
hell exhales

The rotors purr
blades slice the thick blue sky
the smoke charged jungle air
passes away
all that is burning
is left behind

I feel a weight on my chest
as they cut my clothes away

the Huey leaves the LZ
with a nod to the earth
as small rivers of blood
collect in the corners of the hold
there is some crying
someone is screaming at someone
to get my head inside of the hatch

I lie with my head draped over a shoulder,
my shoulder?
To watch the earth leave below me
My body is being tugged and wrapped
the morphine slides down my spine
like warm fingers
I stop the shaking

———

I am living on tuna fish and cereal
and drink too much
I wander through the classifieds,
I never make work on time,
all complain —
the days stare me down
like a dog guarding its bone

———

Her eyes rest on my face
as if they could touch me
her words come to me
in a chalice

———

I am one ignored glance
away from a solitary, cold room
I am one bullet away from eternity
I keep a loaded 45mm
under my mattress
Rescue
There is a hand under my neck
lifting me away from the door
Rescue
I cannot see the earth
there is nothing but eternity
in her eyes
Rescue

RIVER

a river runs through your eyes
incessant and timeless
coming toward me
a thing that I cannot stop

your voice rises around me
like autumn mountains,
soft yellow and red desire
drifting down on me in a wind,
next to you
there is a vortex where I stand

this moment is a storm
I rub the cuts on my brow
and stand outside the ring
wondering if I can find myself somewhere
in the sound of your voice

I finish a highball
lying on our bed
in this languid heat of summer
and roll over to turn off the lamp
kissing the bed sheet beside me
unconscious of anything I do

RUNNING

I will never run from you
I have not yet met you
I will spend the rest of my life running to you
I see your head just above the hedgerow or
Tilted sideways in your garden
I smell your skin on the sheets beside me
And turn only to have
the curtains billow with empty wind
In the space you have left
I will try to meet you at the warm hearth of
    our home,
This earthly heaven where I retreat
Where I am shaking off the leaves of midlife
But I can still run for desire of you
I can still catch more than your eyes, your
    thoughts,
I can still catch all of you

SLEEPING LIPS

What do your sleeping lips say?
the night bed room
glows from your bright arms
that holds all the secrets of my days

The wind chime sings quietly outside
a dog barks not knowing why
I want the gray light
to stay beneath the earth
I want reason to go to
someone else's morning table

The darkness is mine
The room carries your last whispers to me
they perch on my heart
I will not stir them
the night is watching
I gather up the stars
and make a bed for you
I order the moon to watch over you
and let the inky, sweat blackness
cover me
I will wait for what your sleeping lips will say

SMILE

How this light wraps your smile
I am trying to steal it back
cage it in my heart
before the cold twilight

The evening strokes your face
with moonglow
your smile still rests
in the corner of my arms
the stars have eyes for you
let them burn
hold your breath next to mine
send me the angel of this night
my arms hold you once
heavy enough for forever

SOMETIME AFTER

Locked away in the corner of my eye
is the memory of your laughter
the curve of your neck
and the swell of your breast
in an unbearable repose

The incline of the hill reminds
me that this is not a dream
the sand of Jersey Shore
Seems real enough
For both of us

I carry all these hard packages
in a worn canvas bag
a vagabond in the dunes

I have gained
a life of indifference
yet you are the thought
that comes to my heart this quiet hour
you are the monument of twenty years past
that erupts
to tell me that I am nothing
but a dry shell
on the beach
the creature has left

THE BLOOD LET

I wish you were here
filling my kitchen doorway
the way you did that summer,
your brown gold skin
holding back the light from the outside,
in cloaked stillness,
you would offer you secret silhouette to me
asking for my eyes
you put them in a dark place
holding them with a force
that only silence knows

with the pain of light and remembering
— tomorrow, today —
I watch you gather the corners of your dress
holding them for me
holding the dress only that it could be released
    — a swan bows its head at dusk
the dress falls
as cut petals

when I have run my hands along your throat
I asked, 'where do the lambs die?'
I have their wool now
caught and gathered gray tuffs

is it a soft, warm place with

shallow bleating and blood?
is there acceptance?

their eyes lit on fire with the
slow knowledge of darkness,
a frenetic offering of hooves
raised in the air filled with wood, wool,
    and dust
ages and ages of killing dust
raised in pantomime motion
before this, their blood let

your face, sunk deep
within the room's darkness,
is scalded with wet, black
slashes of your hair
your head turns slowly towards me,
time and I wait behind you

THE FERTILE CRESCENT

The romance
of a Central Park bench,
eyes,
dipped in twilight,
glitter

This could have been
a fishing village
at the great basin
the story of your lovers
flowing like that river,
limpid pools
here at the nameless edge of man's history
the ardor of dark skinned glances,
hallowing the dust beneath the Sphinx's
    silence

through this mist
of a winter's day in Manhattan —
you look back
with no one in a crowd of millions
to notice your posture of eternity
but me

THE FIRST SEASON

The sound of the day sleeper
cough and wrinkles
rolling over the ghosts of
this house with a thousand closets

I scream at the sound of this feeling
driving away
a steel car gripping the rail
of highway
leaving

I can not remember the
way you looked at me
when you drove away
I do not remember
the night or the day
I can not remember
the sky or earth

I only remember the
gentle tug
of a wagon
with tin wheels
squeaking under my brother's weight
the long path to school
in the morning

I am quiet and simple
my lunch money in hand
I have come without fear
innocent of pain
the First season

THE KISS

Simple seven
the sum of my fingers
pressed upon the hollows of your face
enough to allow your smile —
the quiet fading green of your eyes
closed
petal and feathers

Divided lips, felt, velvet, fluted tongue
the crush and roll of these soft angles
a gold clasp gives up the jewel
my breath wrested from me

the blade leaf midnight beauty
rising behind you,
lashes of your hair
stray back in the wind
like so many children's arms
waving goodbye

I approach this memory like an altar

A DIFFICULT MAN

So I want to punch my eye out with a sharp pencil
the geese crash open the surface of the water
by a hair trigger of noise
how am I to be disposed to the rough ends of life?
this moment to forgive,
the stages of the cross
that only to lead me to a knife's edge
screaming inside with a fit
Angry enough to bite the radiator
I am the Roman soldier with a whip
I can't fight, I can scream inside
I am blind in one eye
I blame you, fortune or god,

I have always been a difficult man
I ride some pretty days for all they are worth
Roy Rogers on Trigger, a white steed — rescue
I float about a forgiving universe
still I curse
bad rhymes from a bad man
Let me in, let me do what I can

Not prepossessing or even interesting
no matinée idol, a swamp full of anger and
    loathing
I am the meter of self

I don't pretend that you could walk with me
I have lost the desire to see
I am a crippled in a pure white house

come to me child and wife
do not forsake me
for the terror that I am
forgive me as I am learning to forgive
    myself

DUST

the sheen of morning sun
runs across this table, gloss maple
with a gossamer of dust
the fine trembling rust
I am

waiting for the tender disruption of a door
a window split seam
and I am gone
scattered in Brownian motion
a skeleton plume
mixed about in this room
where I have seen
your glance destroy and create
every piece of me
ever to be lost or found

HALLWAY

The paneled hallway's wainscoting
below a forest green sanded velvet cool
all, the all
leads to you
the doorway at the end of the hall
is the doorway at the end of my day, my life
you and the child beyond

within
this winter interior
the yawning distance to walk —
from my makeshift bed,
the drift of these days,
lying in a noose of pillows
La dolce vita
of late morning awakenings
the self pity and last night's vodka
not enough to sustain me
I look at the shimmering light from the hall
a fractured blur
head down, my face turned right
with my eye not quite right
I have gained the possibility of walking
of return
of seeing you
the bright nova beyond the door
what have I been waiting for?

HOME

Fourty five minutes of battery power remain
in my laptop's recesses
I conclude, on this Friday afternoon,
that
I have more time than thoughts
but I remember the pressure that fumes
    from behind
of work, the coming spring,
the nature of time
all things that I want to see
to walk down Fifth Ave
to hike in 20 knots of wind
to drink espresso in a piazza in Rome,
to roam about your body
and drink your vision
so that I never leave home
I have enough time to stay home

THE PHLEBOTOMIST

she didn't like the water much
she would wait for me before the wake
smiling her quiet smile
she would laugh
and a hundred school children would fill
 the hallways pushing for the bell
and I am driven along with them
as I run out of the water toward her
so that memory turns
as the sand in my palm.
it is time to go home,
try to beat the traffic, eat dinner —
she would never care about these things

"this won't hurt a bit"
something sweet and painful touches me
I hardly notice it at first
she is good at her art and she knows this
the vein folds and
my heart knots
to stop the bleeding
I take the pain for granted

she snaps the tourniquet
and states, "all done"
she bends my arm
and shakes the last tube

rolling the rich, red stuff in her hands
"and what's that one for?" I ask
she looks up at me finally
with a hard press of her eyes
and smiles
"oh, this one? this one's for me."

TRAIN STATION

I am fourteen again
Belligerent lost child, so lonely for your smile
Wanting and wan
County park with quarts of Schlitz beer
it is your voice that I hear

I have left Grove Street
I have assumed life and the fear that parades
in front of my porch
fear that leaves a posting everyday
in the mail box
on the nineteenth century porch
never attended

Forgive me all,
forgive me all that I have done
I will betray you
I will leave, have left you
without turning for a last embrace
without the union of tears left at the station
left without thought
left without you

VAMPIRE

the silver air
the man in a dinner jacket
diffident posture,
immaculate and listening
his uniform is life
forgetting his tombstone just for one moment
the cold of January howls outside

the moon was captured into this scene
full and glowing beyond imagination
it reels up
like a Satyr
raising its head from the field after the rape

the figure of the gloved hand
splashed in moonlight
bone white fingers
with vermilion nails
curled to beckon the innocent
open and caressing
my cheek beneath her palm

I look at the moon —

my head is wrenched back
with a the suddenness of a slap
I hear the soft, muffled crush
I am dead before she begins

the blood she covets
is given willingly, without notice

WHAT I FOUND TODAY

I found my son's smile today
as bright as a western sun and warmer still
I found my friends
I found the soft sift of autumn grass
the brilliant ocean, foam, ever ready surf
I found the truth of the day
the wisdom of the word
I found love, again,
in the sweet hollow
of my wife's withered shoulder
I found god today
at the end of a long, thin tether

But there he was.

YOU CAN NOT IMAGINE

you can not imagine
the fragrance
of these cut lillacs
cut fresh in spring
without a thought
of you
antique white
and velvet blue
outside my window
without a thought of you
cut stem
in full bloom
you will wonder
at the warmth of summer
without a care
crystal ivory petals
set against my eye
far from you

Other Poems

AMPHIBIAN

So easy to feel
feel this way
The fires settles in a soft crush
you didn't expect

The cool liquor of forbidden Sunday
in Connecticut
The cat who counts the seconds
for the end of the music
that lathers the room

The sun is reconciled to the earth
the creek is ablaze with the fire
this is the last offering of the evening
god rests in this place,
rests in my heart

ANACONDA

There is no bottom
this night air is dry, and thin
Sleepless
the page held against the light

In the valley of the blind
the one eyed jack holds court
The serpent coils
The long sleep
The S awaits, sleeps
A charm, a potion, a way out

The anaconda takes one wrap
the smothering should stop soon
S, the long sleep

ANOTHER ANTIGONE

Another Antigone
stands over me
gathers my bedsheets beside me
so that the lips of soft edges brush over each
    other —
lovers coming awake, coming apart,
morning, the embrace of self,
the longing for all this, soft material life
in a vortex of cotton and wool

she comes upon me while I am near the edge
    of sleep,
doped with fatigue and dreams —
the canopied green of our childhood backyard
the soft rot of that 19th century house
and the riot of six children slowly adding to
    its elegant decay
the dreams of summer with you, mom, Tony,
    Alex, Christine And John,
of coke bottles and greasy French fry bags
of easels and oil paint and
water colors and paper
and large summer hats that only she could
    wear, now perhaps, you
her smile and laughter are your inheritance —
as am I,
your lowly brother of numbers and pain,

of storms and tribute,
responsible and unapproachable,

I do not plead for you
I do not beg for you
I never had to
My Antigone

AUTUMN

One life is found upon these rocks
green gravel and grass at low tide, the Sound
    is full of room
there is an order to the universe and then
there is not
the sun is hot for this season
the moon casts a glance homeward

I turn to John to ask him about my adventure
I want to leave and go south of the border
to heat the engine of a used car until it makes
    steam
to walk in the heat after peyote and beer
to fall into the barren patch of earth until the
    storm
in me ceases
and I return

"I'll do it."
and I know that he would, ignorant of my
    quest for ruination
but with a gentle clutched hand around my heart

I have walked this jetty all day with him
waiting for a run of striper or blues,
nothing but bottom fish,
nothing off the lures that we have casted

a thousand thoughtless times
casted over this last pale sunset of the
    amber, failing,
hazed autumn

allowing us back to our homes
of meals and compromise
thoughts of you, our sea,
and thoughts of you our wind, sun, and moon
thoughts of you, our season
before you leave

CHALMERS STREET

the courtyard picks up a breeze
mounting to a wind
carrying scraps of *the Tribune*
held in a twist
a silent dance, never to be repeated
in front of this house
fourteen rooms and the lovers walk by

fourteen rooms
a child's cry begins above,
caresses a door's side, slides
down the stairs, over the banister
and along the wainscot —
to a door, but never beyond the hearth

one million cries
one million laughs set off
by brighter eyes, small blue nova's,
shining beacons
in this deep pool of home

one million nods
one million sighs caught up
in a blanket of stars that move
like a woman's hands across your back

one million tears
one million winks

and what of these?

the stop lights at the corner of Halsted
    and Lincoln

cannot stop the river that soars through

these windows a million, million times

how many calls from above?

how many thoughts to loosen

how many ideas to divide

the bouncing, browsing of dogs

the pecking steps of a child

the light pounding of boys

the open mind march of their elders

caped in blond

all their eyes role out and the wonder,
    the wonder

of this place becomes

the idea

the dream

life and its memory

CHILD
for Izze

Let this figure of a child
bare the weight of
tomorrow's light
caught on tree limbs
she is swinging over
old dry heads
which crane slowly upward
to catch the last illumination
between the leaves and her laughter

CHILDHOOD

the turning of the old, silent man
behind
the take-out counter

his eyes light on another
place
other seas, and skies,
other's eyes
I am guessing at his rhythms
I am guessing at his pain

He will not turn
nor turn again —
The boys,
Jimmy, Chris, Liam and Tom,
skating over the earth
sun burnt, windswept, anointed in dirt,
the playing fields that are eternal
when we breath as children
we breath heaven

reading the order —
all the warm, steaming food
one arm reaches to the right,
the other to the left —
Vishnoo illuminates her terror

The Buddha offers me suffering
Christ, tears of the Passion Play,
why am I crying over Chinese food?

Gather me to these thorns of midlife
but how I remember when
my days were bright things
offered to any one
taken by none
memory grows in this blood of time

COLE DEWALD

Cole Dewald
Was born in the fall
He was a fine baby
But unsure of it all
Saying, "Maybe
I'll come into this world
And bring joy to my parents
Who love me most —
That is apparent —
Or maybe for the rest of this life
I'll leave and become errant
A child of the world"
"Oh but you can't"
Said his mother and father
Stay here and live by our side
Don't wander the world,
That such a long ride,
Be our loving little boy,
Please stay and abide

So Cole Dewald
Answered the call
of the song that his parent's sung
noting that while they
may grow aged and gray
their love for him
will always be young

DANCERS

this poem willows in the wind
a hard currency to sell
the plague of reason
from the video screens stares at me

life comes in through
the port holes
slowly, beneath the notice
of the dancers on deck
who are waiting for the band

DEAD GRASS

How I would relish that blood in my mouth,
to sallow you whole and save you from this
    mountain of pain
to save the vision of yourself
that you have held
like the small girl that you were once
cradling a doll with doll eyes

to suck, with all my power, with every seam
    within me
drawn into an unholy knot —
to will this bloodlet
out of a small quarter of your brain
and let you sleep
to sleep with me and be my love,
again
again

The flood came last Sunday
A rising tide across the street that breached
    the berm
and made us as one with the Long Island Sound
the lawn is an uncomfortable shade of yellow
the quince, hydrangeas and azaleas all rust
    with the salt
the withering touch from the sea
the great mother who has borne us all
returns to remind

DEATH

the window
begins the morning
the heather teases the wind
I think over my newspaper to where
I might begin again
over loft,
over the rain ridden road
the car screams off the shoulder
time nurtures a moment in terror
to die this death perhaps every day

DETACHMENT DEFERRED

Head down, head down,
the photopsia rains in my eye
I see you in the left quarter panel
I am lucky to see any quarter panel
Head down the doctor says, head down
perhaps I can kill the electric butterfly today,
it has been a month already
I can see my son's lips through the pneumatic
    retinopexy, the bubble
kill the butterfly, kill the butterfly

This is an annoying decision,
no not a decision, bow
bow your head,
bow your head in pain
bow your head in acceptance
bow your head in humility
the loss of sight in a single eye is insignificant
remind yourself of gifts
that could be taken from you
the earth that could be taken from you
remind yourself of the love that has been
bestowed upon you
without hesitation,
given freely, for you

All may be taken
any minute these may be taken
and you would still be richer than
you could have ever dreamed
you can dream
this could be taken
dream
live this dream
become this dream
your are the dream
forget your sight
you can see

FATHER

Oh my father,

Aged, lovely, crippled thing

Let me gather you in my arms like you once
    held me

Let me look into your eyes, broke and blue as
    the end of the day

Join me on this green playing field

On this winter white slope

The strange laughter of your five children
    who mock and adore you

How this life never ended,

how childhood was never a stage,

but everything, every time, everywhere,
    always then, now, and tomorrow

Who says goodbye and means it,

Who?

GOD

chanting and ranting
that is the residue of today,
not much different form yours, I am sure
but could there but something,
somehow different here in the suburbs
I have heard of the Dali Lama
I have heard of the Ecstasy
The release of desire
the Passion Play that
haunts my days
I am not worthy to receive you, oh my lord
the kites of spirit that sing through the air
around my house, my despair,
the dervishes twirl
all spin around me
so that I am almost
found
while so lost at sea

GRACE ON A SUMMER'S EVENING

The grace of the evening
Given to me before vespers,
a small acknowledgement from You of your
    beneficence

While strained with a headache all afternoon —
Holding her left forehead below the suture line,
She cupped this buldge with right her hand
The gray pall of her face, of this afternoon
Erases the ease of my life, our life together,
Our friends, their children playing on the
    lawn with our child
In this glorious day filled with a shocking blue sky
and a northwest wind that taste like ice cream
    cake
— It is so heavenly it must be you

GOO GOO THE GORILLA

Goo Goo the gorilla
Sits on his pilla
Quiet, with nothing to say
The animals behind him
Press to remind him
To shout loud, for this is Cole's birthday!

But Goo Goo the gorilla
Remains very stilla
Not moved to outburst is he
He knows that excitement
Will not bring the enlightenment
Found beneath the quiet Bode tree

"But he is such a happy boy"
Scream your other animal toys
"He needs to run, to jump, to PLAY"!
Though all remonstrate
Goo Goo will not abdicate
The quiet throne of happiness from which
    he reins

Though you may be a rough boy at first sight
The cat runs you from you in fright!
And days of easy sunshine
will fall on your brow
thinking and reading
Are the paths to receiving
The most precious gifts god will allow

TO GRANT MOORE

Grant Moore, Grant Moore
What the heck are you crying for?
You will chide me for that dangling participle
For I know you are a child of great principle
But your loud vocalizations
belie your frustrations
You are leveled to prostration
You have settled with indignation
after having left the sacred womb of certainty
— another candidate for immortality —
Aloof, august, austere,
Your baby pink face has never shown fear
Now as you have entered the world
in a noisy high gear

But why is this?
Why are you somewhat trembling in your bearing,
Do you feel your relatives staring?
Are they are pinching and coddling?
And ohhing and ahhing
Attempting to restrain you with baby swaddling
Oh the indignity
You suffer at the hands of such lesser beings
You who deign to compliment this mere soup
      of dirt and air
You who has set your baby foot down where
the earthly ground then becomes sacred

Blessed, noble, beyond compare,
You are laid low now — it is so unfair
You must now descend
from your epistemological highs
you have been humbled,
your diapers have been rumpled
you can not comprehend your bad luck
For you have been given the last name,
    Ignatuk

Like some primordial link,
Australopithecus
You have been made to look ridiculous
It starts with the Ig of ignominy and
and then falls off the tongue like a boulder
    to the sea
no pride or elevation
only teary eyed lamentations
You could have been a Vineyard or Jones
But you have been left in your crib to moan
Your name will make you seem plebian
or something vaguely eastern European

And though you may come to walk
    though life
To prove your superiority again, and again,
And though you may someday walk the
    quad of U Penn
Though you may cover your walls with
    blue ribbons and loving cups

It will never seem enough
Always beaten down with the name:
   Grant Moore Ignatuk

GREY'S CREEK

I look out at this tidal creek at sunset
with the cooing morning doves on the
    telephone wire
blushed pink, what do ya think?
I continue to read until twilight
I have forgotten to look up
and now it is night

The days ebb and flow
the cedar mist of morning
the glory of sunlight in the east
the hope
the hope of today
the expectant hatch of spring
with a thousand different duns in the thing

That turns into night
I look up and see
the blur of cars beyond the creek
seen from blear eyes
turned from blue
One thousand British soldiers
could not turn me
from this vision at night
a blank eye
but an open mind
I want to be buried with a gravestone aside
    the eelgrass
let me live at the edge

HARROW

gaining the quiet harrow
carried across the black dirt
with a mule that carries one hundred years
of family
and wind against sheets on a line

worn faces of the farm
silent in a Sunday repast
gather about the table
where corn, pork, sun tea dominate

white gables,
the spring of time
I could have walked there
and been somebody,
something so different

HIGHWAY

Screeching steal and diesel
I95 stumbles to a crawl before Norwalk
a clear morning light threads itself
between one semi and another

I can not see the Sound or sun
except at intervals when traffic begins
and the trucks spread out
for these brief moments
I see the azure December blue
the quiet waving of limbs
from trees by the highway

Is there a god?
The traffic stalls,
I sit in the shadow of a bus

KIND

Well I have thought about it
about the single cold steel barrel
approximate to my adenoids
so that I can choke on something other
    than words
the gush of pain and the blood that would
    be smeared
across my off white, barren bedroom walls

I would dress in an Italian suit, plain but styled
humming tunes before I go
maybe a Coltrane album screaming in the
    background —
the cat would be fearful; I'd have to keep him
    in the other room
with enough food for a while

I offer the threads of my existence ever day
I am strung on a line tethered from me to a
    dry mooring
I look into every eye and see animal never
    word, never kind
I am neon braced on the brink
a push to become a shattering small explosion
    of pink, blue and powder

I can see the Indian paper boy

steal away from the apartment hearth in
the morning

I ask out loud for continuance, for the
rapture of bodies, all bodies,

young, old, fat, green, blessed and illicit

to scream and roll over me in sleep

to whisper out some poor, lonely song in
an indifferent ear

before they dissipate with a feeling they'll
call love

and I will try to agree because I am
happier for it

I want to take a deer

to bleed it in a dark wood

beneath trees that wave soft autumn flags
of yellow and hectic red

covered with killing blood

resting

LEAVING HOME

The rhythm of weeds in the wind goes still
the pigeons wait at the window sill
for the window that does not open
the flat light of morning that has come

Shadows dance in the alley ways
the bums cough and puke
in front of the mission
the smell of piss in all corners

these sweet tendrils of earth
that lace our shoulders
as we are ready to turn
are slow to slip —
the crush of hands,
the caress at the bus stop,
the frenetic wave from a passing window —

A scruff dog scratches a bleeding ear,
nozzles a dry crotch,
dodges a car on Vanhouten Street
then sniffs the air —

Something new, something new, something new
a tail wags in paradise

LET

So that I am in this wonder lust of the outside
together with a thought of winter land
the carbon coolness of New Jersey in
    December
after the fall
after the rut
called from a wire extending down from ages,
ages and ages
how all the seams of life
collect together hear at the edge of wood
a billion years deep
I ask for union
I smell the silence of this past season
and see the deer as they run through a
    crimson menagerie
fall, fall
dawn turns a golden handle

LIGHT

how much light exits
from this throng, casted off
the dusty edges of crumpled peeling blinds
that I am alone
that I wish for nothing
that jazz rings through my ears
while the outside embraces the cool
of the mountain cottage
before crimson morning
I inhale
and let out thirty years of wonder
could this be the beginning?

MARGARET ANN

Margaret Ann walks to the river
gathering herself, time and flowers
as she goes
entering a spot where the trees break
and the sun pours down in one
golden ribbon
She bows to the reflections
of spawn and seedling
of leaf and petal —
root and arbor
time and her children
the sun reverberates
off this cunning surface
and the earth is abuzz with life above

These small diamond fantails —
their break and fold —
mold to change with the current
and nest against her eye
like so many leaves
that press the river's surface
and are changed
from the instant of their dying fall
to this, a dance of imagination

She kneels beside the river
caught within a cage of form

MY HISTORY

This low, flat light in an autumn morning
Paints a vivid world that I once knew
The mist rising off the surface of a quiet
  pond,
The trees boughs move in *Adagio*
This all occurred sometime in my history
With these leaves dipped in gold and crimson
The slow movement of props in a play after
  the actors have left
This is a closet left open for me to look into
  without rejoicing
There is no matter in the thing, no blue guitar
here stories have been told and retold until
  the past is mocked into silence
Its beauty forgotten, pictures in a hallway
Come today, see me again,
Come today, all this light will be here waiting
  for you and me

NIGHTDAY

The shadow of roses
colored by moon paint
flicker nervously
on a quiet midnight floor
dry boots to walk over them
outside, this soft night air

Children at the corner
stomp and pull at their clothes
looking for the hectic yellow engine
mothers waiting with the radio,
peer through a car window
a bright wave
the dog slumps against the backseat
— goodbye!

A gull is caught on the wicked blue of the sky
the sea is rimmed with jewels and ermine —
sparkling
the waves thunder in a circle
all around me

POMPEY HOLLOW

The crease of asphalt that rides across the
  spine of Pompey Hollow
pressed by the hill and the plain,
pressed by the dumb lick of green earth,
the consumptive life of rebirth
pinwheels to catch their heels to the wind,
  hatch the rhythm
that stung and fooled every cowboy, saint and bug
since the dawn of time
into Life
into this gorgeous arbor

This sweet holy bliss,
these renegade tracts of desire
that leads again and again
to the primordial earth
the deep ravine
the rushing spring water

the last hope
of the beginning of desire
the beginning of life
the end of all knowing
the end of all attempts

to piece the fire together
and the thousand, thousand dreams to come,
no one knows how much so

the need for a figure at dawn
the need for a figure, a night
the words that rest in the face of time's
    children
all come again

ROWING TOWARDS GOD

how hard to open these wide seas
wide as children's eyes before desire
to allow hearts,
all hearts, however broken and small,
a gentle path
in this constant rowing
towards God

SHOULDER

The bright day
the rueful twilight
all of these passages through time
end on a jagged edge, the spire catching a
    shoulder
the frozen stare from the elevator
I have just choked on this capsule
it will make this day right
the sun goes down
light to my shoulders
my god, I have to run,
my god

STAY TUNED

Stay tuned
Stay tuned
This is tomorrow
Tommorow's afternoon
You can guess what I am thinking
you may think I have been drinking
Stay tuned
stay tuned
I promise you nothing
exactly what you have been expecting

STREAM

these river rocks are
so hard

I can not stop
the constant flowing
of this stream
that runs to me

SUMMER

the clothes line sings
the sheet cotton white smelling of the daisies
    and green grass
snaps in the wind
like a slow jazz man keeping a soft beat
of a song that he seems to be forgetting

the children stretch their thin brown arms
hands clasped above
reaching behind their heads and smiling like
    sin itself —
a prayer issued backwards
waiting in the early morning summer heat
for no one in particular
rusted street sign, dust, and laughter
the cicadas work up their machinery
the heat rises

and the back yard is paint and color and a
    squawking clothes line
it is a mother leaning out with clothes pins in
    her mouth
dedicated to this one chore
with an eye to the corner

SUMMER'S END

this sorrowful sea
that levels yesterdays against
the back porch of your heart
so that summer is gathered
in a basket
the billow of white bed sheets
tethered closer to your day than you realized
fresh, pale days
sundrenched and lost
of their salted balm
of beach fronts and their jagged picket of
    food stands
the tepid, torrent promise from eyes
of candy colored girls
offering ice cream
across stainless steel counters
with smiles that nearly
break the countenance of your life

a dying song passes in front of my eyes,
I drive away —
lemon sweet their skin,
brilliant pearly eyes and red lips —
all fecund promise
all wet caramel rimmed glances
faded, blanched against this sheet in a
    summer breeze

color washed to the tone of wind and ash
soft is this final parade

TEA CUP

I have given
some thought to those small realities
waiting outside
the window flower box
caught like in a photographer's flash
the dull moment
before my mocking bird's cry —
how can I explain?

life at the bottom of a tea cup

TEENAGE WASTELAND
for Maureen

I consider the bright future
what will happen to me
enrich me, imbue me with a happiness
that can not be measured by
yesterday's standard

I am filled with yesterday
I try to look at tomorrow, its promise
but I am leaking
from fissures in my soul
and every thought that splits my seams, seems
to be filled with you, all of you

Carried before me at breakfast and following me
like hungry cats in the alley
I turn to these thoughts —
a lunch box, third row, second seat at St. Paul's
the smell of autumn, grass caught in my
    face guard
a street full of children,
a desk full of books,
the lawn with noise and joy
your lost and found looks
that you could speak to all of it

if I could spill
all these dreams that surround me every
    evening, everywhere
beneath a golden harvest moon
making arrangements with myself?

Painted with pale moon paint
County park is electric
You are fourteen and eternal
how many quarts of Schlitz beer can you drink
and what has been created without thought
without ever understanding
becomes the weight of what I will carry
everyday thereafter through life
everywhere you turn, there is the face of god
everywhere I turn there you are

there are bell bottoms and Indian cotton
    blouses
there are smiles, breast, books, and
    teacher's looks
there is Madison Square Garden
the Passaic
the Forum
and the numbered seats in empty rows
the Blarney Stone outside the Garden
and how would I know that I would
    become 50
how could I possibly know what would fit
    me tomorrow
when I was fourteen

But I am fourteen and the world is a cauldron
   of love and promise
I promise I will be home by midnight
I promise that I will understand

THE BUDDHA FALLS

The Buddha falls
from its place on a suburban book shelf
four hundred years it rests on
bronze shoulders
in Cambodia

stripped and torn
making flight in a gunny sack to Vietnam
sold on a street in Saigon
carried to the States
by a soldier turned artist

given to me when the artist
throws all his possessions away
to live in Maine
after his wife left him

carried by me from upstate NY
to NY city, to Chicago, to Connecticut
to rest on a shelf
next to liquor bottles and photographs
my coveted relic
ancient, timeless —
falls to a terracotta floor
I let go

THE ENDING

Now: I am clinging to blue of your eyes
The dry rattle of your bones in a purse of
    paper skin
To every grunt of welcoming from your bed,
every cough of your laughter,
every clutch of my arm
every demand for my strength

Then: Every frat boy beery smile and every
    young man brag,
every howl and cheer from the bleachers,
Every shake, every shout that tied the ecstasy
    of turning the boy to the man

Then: every stroke of my crew cut,
every rule, every scolding —
all ending in your arms on your warm chest
Carried from the back seat, carried from the
    couch, carried from the neighbor's house,
Carried across the yard, from school, from
    college, from work, from today,
To this bed where you lay past tomorrow,
    beyond yesterday

Now: I am going to cling to
this borrowed life,
I'm going to scrape my fingers against this
    rich peal of earth,

Fill my hands with your soil
I will not let go
As I am dragged to the sea,

To the blue memory of your eyes
Then crushed upon the shore
To be drawn back in the ebb and now
Crushed once more

THERE

There
the clouds and clowns have given way
there
the seas have turned to the warm earth
blankets of blue
there
the mountains caress air with
the passion of meadow larks with wing against
  the wind
there
the calamity of the street is taken
into some back room and kindly talked to
there
the fire bursts at your feet, every day, every where

TOMORROW

The child tussled a hundred times over
an overheated, fat limbed fugitive
searching for the refuge, deep into the evening
bounded in a plastic crib
he digs his head into a pillow
as a rugby player in a scrum
looking for the end of consciousness
the end of the day
the promise of evening's dreaming
the morrow to come

T V

The promise of seventies tv
how much that meant to me
the psychology of men and their children
stars upon a ceiling
don't cry

VG MOVING

The morning's frost not quite gone and the
    air with the bite of fall
You ramble up the brick path, heavier than
    you looked last year
Carrying my 18th century, tiger maple highboy
What a delight!
This air breathed by so many men:
    Paracelsus, Occam, Augustine, the sons of
    the Revolution,
And now you and me panting on the front stairs
I rub my face against my new gift of history

WIND

the clue of the head sail leaps out
and spills an indifferent wind
the Sonnars gather at the favored pin
and the gulls scream before the gun

the main and the jib luff in the breeze
as profanities fill the air
as the peace of the blue gives way to this,
race day

the slow rock of the tide
entering the Long Island Sound
the cares lost at the dock,
stepping onto the launch,
are replaced by the joy of wind -
water covers my life.

WINTER'S DAY

Buffleheads and mergansers dress the pond
February is here, almost gone
the cedar needles soak in winter's parfait
I have given all my sight to the creek
I consider a walk to the water's edge
but decide to stay
a feathered couch, a useless man

The day leaves me
sumptuous and pale,
everything I own
is in the line of sight
from my living room
my wife, my child
my future that may leave soon
I can not reconstruct the pastels of light and color
that has surrounded my neglectful attention
family bliss, forest rectitude — the lovers,
what am I to do in this state between?
the sense of now
and the fear of other

The blind lead out their children
and help them with the acceptance of the
    future's cold
they lean upon their soulful looks,
and weave for them a soulful prayer

their vision is held within a lifetime of
    certainty
that the coffee pot on the counter
is where it should be
and the rooms at Holiday Inns don't
    ever change

We depend on the common things that
    construct
an ordinary life
we caste our wings into an expectant flight
but recall the book that reassures our right
to settle here in the suburbs
to discuss the mornings weather
when it so obvious
that we are all together

YOUR FACE

I lay my hand on your sleeping skin tonight
the soft baby curl of your lips
the saintly pause of your face in sleep and
    darkness
are too beautiful to describe

I am twenty three
kneeling in front of my mother's casket
her full rouged face is too beautiful to describe
it holds years of memory's triumphs
it is at once transcendent and dead
I touched her cheek and I am brought back to
    my age

I will try to hold these links
the generations that step from one decade
onto the next
timorous fear in movement,
await the footfall
your father comes
quiet, my beautiful son,
your father comes

Lightning Source UK Ltd.
Milton Keynes UK
UKHW051348121019
351348UK00012B/129/P